YOU KNOW YOU'RE A VET TECH IF YOU'VE...

A FUNNY ADULT COLORING BOOK

TAKE AN ART THERAPY BREAK FROM A CHAOTIC DAY AT THE VET CLINIC & HAVE SOME FUN WITH YOUR WORK FRIENDS BY COLORING EACH PAGE YOU CAN RELATE TO!

THANKS FOR CHOOSING A GRACE WINTER COLORING BOOK. WE TRULY HOPE THE RECIPIENT OF THIS BOOK GETS A FEW LAUGHS FROM THE QUOTES INSIDE. AS A SMALL BUSINESS SELLING ON AMAZON, YOUR FEEDBACK IS IMPORTANT TO US. WE WOULD APPRECIATE IT IF YOU COULD TAKE A MINUTE TO POST AN HONEST REVIEW ON AMAZON.

YOU KNOW YOU'RE A VET TECH IF YOU'VE...

NEVER HAD A QUIET
DAY AT WORK

YOU KNOW YOU'RE A VET TECH IF YOU'VE...

HAD A
PATIENT
THAT WON'T KEEP
STILL DURING A
CATHETER
PLACEMENT

YOU KNOW YOU'RE A VET TECH IF YOU'VE...

STAYED UP LATE
THINKING
ABOUT YOUR
PATIENTS

YOU KNOW YOU'RE A VET TECH IF YOU'VE...

HAD A CONVERSATION
WITH A CLIENT
THAT FELT LIKE IT WOULD
NEVER END

YOU KNOW YOU'RE A VET TECH IF YOU'VE...

BECOME A
MASTER
AT
MULTI-
TASKING

YOU KNOW YOU'RE A VET TECH IF YOU'VE...

REPEATED YOURSELF
MULTIPLE TIMES IN
ONE CONVERSATION

YOU KNOW YOU'RE A VET TECH IF YOU'VE...

NEVER GONE
A DAY WITHOUT
CLEANING UP POOP

YOU KNOW YOU'RE A VET TECH IF YOU'VE...

CONSUMED ABSURD
AMOUNTS OF
CAFFEINE
DURING YOUR SHIFT

YOU KNOW YOU'RE A VET TECH IF YOU'VE...

BEEN
GIVEN MORE
RESPONSIBILITIES
AFTER BEING
PRAISED FOR
DOING A
GREAT
JOB

YOU KNOW YOU'RE A VET TECH IF YOU'VE...

STAYED TILL LATE
AT THE CLINIC

YOU KNOW YOU'RE A VET TECH IF YOU'VE...

LEFT THE OFFICE
COVERED IN URINE
AND SCRATCHES

YOU KNOW YOU'RE A VET TECH IF YOU'VE...

BEEN CURSED
WITH A
FAULTY
IV PUMP

YOU KNOW YOU'RE A VET TECH IF YOU'VE...

HAD A CLIENT
REFUSE
TO PAY

YOU KNOW YOU'RE A VET TECH IF YOU'VE...

FELT ITCHY AFTER
WORKING ON AN
ISOLATION PATIENT

YOU KNOW YOU'RE A VET TECH IF YOU'VE...

BEEN ON THE
VERGE OF A MELTDOWN

YOU KNOW YOU'RE A VET TECH IF YOU'VE...

BEEN BANNED FROM TELLING WORK STORIES AT DINNER

YOU KNOW YOU'RE A VET TECH IF YOU'VE...

ACCIDENTALLY
STABBED
YOURSELF

YOU KNOW YOU'RE A VET TECH IF YOU'VE...

BEEN
VERBALLY
ATTACKED
BY A CLIENT

YOU KNOW YOU'RE A VET TECH IF YOU'VE...

FELT
GUILTY
FOR
LEAVING ON
TIME

YOU KNOW YOU'RE A VET TECH IF YOU'VE...

WRESTLED
A PUG FOR A
NAIL TRIM

YOU KNOW YOU'RE A VET TECH IF YOU'VE...

HAD TO TELL A CLIENT
"THOSE ARE NIPPLES
NOT TICKS"

YOU KNOW YOU'RE A VET TECH IF YOU'VE...

HAD A
"NEUTER
YOUR PET"
TALK

YOU KNOW YOU'RE A VET TECH IF YOU'VE...

HEARD THE WORD
"SPADED"

THANKS FOR CHOOSING A GRACE WINTER COLORING BOOK. WE TRULY HOPE THE RECIPIENT OF THIS BOOK GETS A FEW LAUGHS FROM THE QUOTES INSIDE. AS A SMALL BUSINESS SELLING ON AMAZON, YOUR FEEDBACK IS IMPORTANT TO US. WE WOULD APPRECIATE IT IF YOU COULD TAKE A MINUTE TO POST AN HONEST REVIEW ON AMAZON.

Made in United States
Cleveland, OH
30 August 2025

19935284R00031